Destierro Means More
than Exile

Gracias, Charles,
for your poems

MARÍA LUISA ARROYO

that embody observations
of nature, of the
"human condition,"
of the lives
before our eyes
if we have the courage
to really see

10·26·19   María Luisa Arroyo

FOREWORD

As a volunteer poet for the May 2018 30/30 Project for Tupelo Press, I challenged myself to write new poems daily and raise money for an independent press that published two collections by one of my mentors, the poet Margaret Szumowski (1949-2013). The 32 women poets who have influenced me - and continue to influence me - as a poet and teacher of poetry served – and continue to serve - as lightning rods for my imagination.

Every morning, as I revisited their collections of poems, I generated drafts on unlined paper until I found them finished enough. Part of this fascinating process included the form, shape, and line breaks each poem demanded after the raw material was on the page.

Once the poem was finished enough, I emailed it to each poet and to Tupelo Press. For those who have passed away, I hope to honor them with my work. In all instances, I want to demonstrate the possibility of fostering literary community - my joyful work for 15+ years – at the same time as I build my literary citizenship.

I intentionally kept the order of the poems in alphabetical order by the poet who inspired it. As you read these poems, find your own instances of resonance in each one and between them.

-María Luisa Arroyo, M.F.A., M.A.

mlarroyo67@hotmail.com
https://www.facebook.com/marialuisa.arroyo.52
https://www.linkedin.com/in/mar%C3%ADa-luisa-arroyo-65035742/

ACKNOWLEDGMENTS

I want to thank Meg Kearney, Founding Director, of the low-residency Solstice M.F.A. Program at Pine Manor College; my poetry peers who are my family; all the teaching poets in this program; and Solstice peers and writers in other genres for the inimitable sense of belonging and support I received [July 2013-July 2015] and that defines the Solstice way.

Why Solstice? As a discerning mid-career professional, I knew exactly what I wanted and what I didn't. Meg Kearney offered me the opportunity to visit the campus to experience the Solstice writing community firsthand, to feel the culture, and to determine whether or not my research/theory that THIS program with such a diverse faculty would provide fertile ground for me and my code-switching poems. The buddy system offered me a fruitful way to ask clarifying questions. Those, who know me, know that I never give false praise and that I do not practice blind loyalty. I not only received an amazing return on my investment in my low-residency Solstice MFA program, I gained a permanent, mutually beneficial writing community.

contents

breaths

for Janet Aalfs

at 47, I re-
turned to my body
through breaths
belly deep, not frantic
moths caught
in my throat

pre-procedure
doctors called it
achalasia
I named it pillo
de mis sueños
& suspiros
thief of my dreams
& sighs
the recliner, my bed

now at 50, I breathe
belly deep
to sing

comelibros: the girl who eats books

for Kathi Aguero

Kids in school & on my street nicknamed
me "The Brain". Where their backpacks
slacked, mine swelled with books
from two libraries, some stamped "obsolete",
mine to keep. Mami called me "comelibros",
the girl who ate books. Abuela feared me,
whispered "loca", my appetite for books
matched her son's, an urban hermit in Puerto Rico.
He crammed towers of books into his head.
Words gushed out his mouth – non-stop.
I live in my head to protect my body.

cruelty

for Ai

In 2018, the youth rage against empty prayers, guns,
$\qquad$ more cruelty.
No place safe for children, for Black men. Our country, open
$\qquad$ sore of cruelty.

With this president, masks fall. The KKK, Neo-Nazis, white
angry men march, their minds twisted to the core with cruelty.

Trayvon Martin. Michael Brown. Renisha McBride. Eric Garner.
Cops did not see the God in them, aimed for cruelty.

Decimated by Spaniards, Taíno traces survive only in maternal
blood & words. Hurakán, storm god who roars with cruelty.

In your poems, Ai, no angels, no wounded healers. Hurt lives,
hate breaks, sex devours. Souls here? You tore out of cruelty.

When the professor jokes that the hurricane has my name,
I say: I have family there. Thank you for your cruelty.

racism   puerto rico   1955

for Elizabeth Alexander

male riders on mopeds & bikes
one to steer
one to slash
with razors, switchblades
the butts of blackbrown women
their god-given bodies & gaits
under long cotton dresses
lustful
see the cotton bleed
see the baskets spill sheets
don't see
the women
as human

Protection

for Naomi Ayala

Broad-shouldered brown men, hands thick
      with work, turn their backs, shields against
your poisoned darts the moment
      they stream in for Saturday coffee.
Behind them, I watch you scan each one, settle
      on the silent man before me in line. You bore
a hole in his left shoulder. It smolders.

Standing taller, I, his round, brown Boricua sister,
      catch your gaze, do not waver,
the privileges of my degrees tilt my head up.
      The soulfire in my eyes burns your retinas,
my floating copper scarf, my "Buenos días",
      more shields for my brothers, hands thick
with work.

la protección

para Naomi Ayala

Hombres con hombros anchos, manos duras
        con el trabajo, sus espaldas, escudos
contra las flechas venenosas de tus ojos
        el momento que entran para comprarse
el buchito de café. Detrás de ellos, te observo.
        Tú escaneas cada uno, decides perforar
-tus ojos, balas - el hombro recto del hombre callado
        en fila en frente de mi. Su hombro arde.

Más alta que él, yo, su hermana Boricua gordita
        y trigueña, atrapo tu mirada, no vacilo,
los privilegios de mis grados de educación
        hacen mi cabeza inclinar hacia arriba.
El fuego de mi alma por mis ojos te quema,
        mi bufanda de cobre, mis "buenos días",
más escudos para mis hermanos, sus manos duras
        con el trabajo.

añorar

para Laure-Anne Bosselaar

añoro, dice mami
       el sabor temblante de la tinglá
           que cazaban mis tíos a la media noche
              yo, 6, desenterraba con mis dedos
                los huevos tremulosos

      las canciones escolares que yo, 10,
           cantaba a la mamá ciega de mi jefa
              yo, un regalo, yo, ya trabajadora
              antes de ser mujer

añoro, dice mami
       la voz de humo de mi papá, su apodo
           para mi, "mi india", mi cabello negro
              un río lacio, mi piel, coco

añoro, dice mami
       pero nunca lloro, mis lágrimas, piedras
           brillantes por dentro, botan chispas
              cuando raspan una contra la otra
              en la boca, la cueva
                de mi secretos

añorar

para Laure-Anne Bosselaar

añoro, says Mami
        the trembling taste of the tinglá
                that my uncles hunted at midnight
                        I, 6, unearthed with my fingers
                                tremulous eggs

        the school songs that I, 10,
                sang to the blind mother of my employer
                        I, a gift, already a worker before I
                                became a woman

añoro, says Mami
        Papá's smoking voice, his pet name
                for me, "mi india", my black hair
                        a straight river, my skin, coconut

añoro, says Mami
        but I never cry, my tears, brilliant stones
                inside me, sparking as they rub
                        in the mouth, the cave of my secrets

Unmasked

for Lucie Brock-Broido, Stonecoast, 1993

LB squared, you flipped up my mask, asked
me to write beyond my eyes, the Hagia Sophia,
Agha-jan's stern face, Mamani's tear-soaked chador,
their son, my husband then, fists of impotent rage
ready to pummel his father for not sending his brothers
into exile during the Iran-Iraq War, slapping me in public
for asking, for not understanding the torrent of Farsi
between father and son, his mother's silence. Let's pose.
The Topkapi Palace, Grand Bazaar, sail up the throat
of Bosporus, eat kebabs, sip chai, sugar cubes gritted
between our teeth, pray to my God, their Allah for mercy.

Visitors

for Lucille Clifton

I don't look for headstones to remember.
My dreamscape is peopled with those
who crossed over, some who stop
to speak with me, others who stride past.
Sometimes, I say, you are in the wrong
person's dream. She lives there, not here.
He has died, too, should be where you are
now. Sometimes, I wait for some to find
a voice, watch their stunned silence
when they open their mouths and
no sound streams out.

They Say

for Judith Ortiz Cofer

They say
when I arrived,
head covered with curls,
the women warned Mami
to cover them with a cap
in Manatí heat
against el mal de ojo.
She listened but
it was not enough.
Mami says
two months into this life
my eyes rolled white,
my tummy ballooned hard
as if filled with river rocks.
Shaking his head, the doctor
sent me home to die.
They say
my aunt bundled up
Mami's grief, took us to see
a woman dressed in white, black
hair flowing up in incensed air.
Mami says
this woman's hands floated
over my prone body, never touched
the taut skin of my jutting belly,
scanned me from head to toe
with prayers in a tongue
Mami did not know.
Mami & aunt say
as my bowels
emptied poison,
my life returned.

Destierro Means More than Exile

for Hilde Domin (1909-2006)

Destierro means more than exile.
Uprooted from. Banished from. Punished
for being deutsche-nicht deutsche, a German

suddenly not German, your mother tongue,
your motherland, no longer yours. Your first flight
with Erwin? Rome. Your second flight?

England. When the U.S. refused to give you visas,
Dictator Trujillo welcomed your whiteness –
three years after he ordered

the massacre of 25,000 Haitians.

Ship-weary, you & Erwin landed. 1940.
Granted 80 acres, 10 cows, a mule & a horse.
Your currency? Your skin. The languages

you taught & translated. The photographs
you took for Erwin, art historian. 1940.
You learn too late of your father's death

in American exile. Vaterlos – no father now
on this island, this ocean, this temporary
life at the edge of suicide. 1951. Your mother

dies in American exile. You learn too late.
Mutterlos, you mouth your Muttersprache, write
your first poems only auf Deutsch, return to

Deutschland with Erwin, change your name
from Löwenstein to Palm to Domin
to remember the choice you made

between suicide and rebirth.

Not Spaniards, July 1898

Manatí, Puerto Rico

for Rita Dove

Papá says the soldiers this time
are not españoles. They march
through town, rifles on shoulders,
some with flags with many white
stars.

Papá tells Mamá to hide our flag
with one star, our hens, keep us
home, especially the boys
who love to play
war.

To Be Loved

for Nicole Terez Dutton

At 5:01 a.m, música wakes the clock radio.
        It sings boleros in the empty bedroom,
                alerts the parakeets of Papi's visit

in dreams. Two years, two months now. Mami sleeps
        in the guest room, its wallpaper, mail-a-prayer flyers
                with Jesus, hazel eyes like Papi's -

imploring. At 73, Mami still wishes to stay, not go.
        Forty-nine years together. Still she feels his orphan's ache,
                Bottomless. Su espíritu. Yearning to be loved.

Whose Hands?

for Diana García

The video praised Hammond's genius, how he built
a replica of a medieval castle, his home. Falso,
Mami said. Whose hands hauled the stone? Cut
& laid each step for staircases that spiral? Plastered
the cooling walls? Swept the steps for cobwebs?
Whose hands built the air for echoes, cathedral
ceiling, hollow walls for this organ's pipes?
Who dusted the inside of each of them? 8,100.
Rubbed to a sheen the metal of empty knights?
Cooked & served beef tongues? Whose hands built
these mosaic-tiled floors, cleaned the spit & vomit
of guests on them as Hammond recounted his joke,
the story about Saint Anthony? Who stood here
silent by the tapestry, pointed out on command
the tongue torn from the saint's mouth?

Whiteness

for Magdalena Gómez

How many times do those who turn to their whiteness.
mistake you for one of them? Your words burn their whiteness.

For years, teachers flattened my tongue into English, mistook
my fluency for assimilation, **their** false yearning for whiteness.

"Borikua mother/[…]/Spanish Father/Taíno beginning/African
soul […]" You unlearned the pressure of whiteness.

For lunch or market runs, I drive extra miles to Springfield, prefer
to shop in peace, not bristle at stares, stern in their whiteness.

2004. Gertrud Kolmar on our lips. Listen to each other's wounds.
Our poems resist the myths, do not mourn whiteness.

Mami's Questions, Translated

for Joy Harjo

Why is only one poet speaking?

When will the poets who are listening have their turn?

Why did so few raise their hand when the poet asked:
How many of you have heard of Sor Juana de Ines?

Where are the poets who look like you?

Why are the poems only in English?

Why are some poets cold and others, warm?

Why did that poet take off his shoes in a room
with no windows, no real air to breathe?

Why did that poet sit on the floor?

Why is your elbow bleeding?
.
Why were the heaters on?

How did this festival choose you?

[Dis]Place[d]

for Meg Kearney

You say, your skin saved you from foster home. You,
                                        condoned in that place.
A family saw you, thin as the wind. Your eyes? Not yet
                                        stones in that place.

I measure my years in dreams. The young girl who still lives there, writes.
Watchful, she has hope on "pause", has outgrown no place.

From "Tattoo": "[…] my bastard's birthmark/ three ravens […]/ stranger
who kept me in her womb." Why were you disowned from that place?

How to erase blood memory? Years later, Papi's orphan ache still gaped.
He over-shopped to give away his love – on loan in this place.

Mami, I wish I could heal the electric storms in your face, sheath nerves.
Matinees make me invisible – no worries. Unknown in this dark place.

Face

for Dorianne Laux

At the poetry festival, you touched a seer: Mami's face.
Your poet's hand read no lines, no fears on her face.

Darkest daughter. Nine = no more school. Cook for white
Ricans, Spanish-speaking like you. Erase here. Your face.

From "Family Stories": what a normal family was like: anger/
sent out across the sill". Words? Spears in her face.

Victoria Fashions, Milton Bradley, Springfield Wire. Factory
work + quotas = finite joy. No children's tears on my face.

A perfect Mother's Day gift?
No stench of beer in our faces.

First Fierce Steps

for Audre Lorde and May Ayim

You inspired Afro-German women poets in Berlin
to take what is theirs: their Germanness, their mother
tongues, their skin, rise up, rise through the corrosive myth
that German=white=purity=go back to where you came from

    | Ich bin von hier.
Wie du bin ich im Mutterleib gewachsen.
Wie du war ich von Brot & Wasser &
       der gedämpften Musik
       einer deutschen Frauenstimme
       ernährt
       die sprach & sang & flüsterte in ihren Träumen
       über mein Werden

Ich gehöre hierher.
Nirgendwo anders.

| I am from here.
Just like you, I grew in a woman's womb.
Just like you, I was nourished with bread & water &
       the muffled music
       of a German woman's voice
       who spoke & sang & whispered in her dreams
       about my becoming.

I belong here.
Nowhere else.

Tongues II

for Demetria Martínez

From kinder, teachers ground their heels into my tongue,
Celebrated my English words, blood congealed on my tongue.

From "Fragmentos/Fragments": "[…] Spanish […] is/ like driving
without hands [….]/ English. My mask, my/sword." Heal your tongue.

Mr. Skala, my Spanish teacher, dislikes my Puerto Rican accent, warns
my peers in Castilian, ignores how my Spanish feels on my tongue.

Post-Hurricane Maria, my brother still dreams of uprooted trees, boxes
of food labeled in English, neighboring elders' appeal for his tongue.

¿El gato asombrerado? ¿Los huevos verdes con jamón? Latinx children
need children's books that look like them, sound real in our tongues.

The Last Bookstore, 1998

for Pat Mora

In the City of Homes, the last bookstore
died. The Mayor did not mourn
it, claimed that all children were reading
on phones & computers. Besides,
who needs to own books when you
can borrow them?

In the City of Homes, a bookstore
desert, children learned to forget
how to read, believed cereal boxes,
billboards, TV screens as cutouts
of their grown-up selves, played
video games to live virtual lives,

forgot to mourn the joy
of reading & writing
their own stories.

Life

for Sharon Olds

Sharon, your wounds live in your poems, rage, tear at this life.
The dark - human, man - no longer a lair in your life.

Unafraid, I redirect the dead in my dreams. Mami is here.
Yes, your sons are safe. No, I still want to wear this life.

Post-Hurricane Maria. Nightmares of flying zinc, uprooted
trees. Awake, my brother, family man, bears this life.

Khosro, more than an Uber driver, speaks about his family
in Iran, desperate economy there, earns fares for their lives.

At Papi's wake. In the receiving line, you whisper: "What
would you do if I hurt your mother?" Dare me to take your life.

Home

for Mary Oliver

The geese guard their nest in the Stop & Shop parking lot.
Why this grassy island curb for home? Was it instinct?
Were they forced off course by April snow? How
do they sense safety? Do they see the cars around them
as boulders in motion? When a grey car slows down,
one goose arches open its wings, leads with its head,
ready to protect. One night, cones appear, set up
a perimeter of safety. Another night, barricades,
two plastic tubs, one with water, the other, oatmeal
and seeds. Imagine such tenderness for new neighbors,
displaced by Hurricane Maria.

hogar

para Mary Oliver

Los gansos hacen su nido
en el estacionamiento de Stop & Shop.
 ¿Por qué esta acera, una isla

de hierba para su hogar? ¿Fue instinto?
¿Fueron forzados desviarse
en las nevadas de abril?

¿Cómo sienten la seguridad? ¿Ven
los carros en su alrededor
como rocas en movimiento?

Cuando un carro gris desacelera,
un ganso tira abierto sus alas,
conduce con su cabeza, listo

para proteger. Una noche aparecieron
conos, crearon un perímetro
de seguridad. Otra noche, barricadas,

dos cubos plásticos, uno con agua,
el otro con abena y semillas.

Imagínate tanta ternura
para vecinos nuevos, desplazados
por el huracán María.

canción

for Dzvinia Orlowsky

When I die, I want Papi's boleros in air. Quémame con su canción.
You say, I burn you with my voice. I say, bésame con tu canción.

After Papi's death, 8 songs are growing in my throat. His orphan's
ache lives in the cuatro chords you play. Tócame esa canción.

1989. To love you again, I sell my violin, fly 3,000 miles. We forget
our mother tongues, our bodies, one. Ámame con nuestra canción.

From "Silvertone": "Father's reaching deep/fingers stretched
into seventh chord/to find his soul." Dzvinia, llórame esa canción.

Mami says she left her first love in Manatí, refused to share his body.
Papi's bass chords stateside, new spiritual balm. Sáname con tu canción.

Twenty-one stories up, your colibri caresses before & after. You want
to meet my son. I refuse, bury this now. Entiérrame con esa canción.

No More Late Bus

for Marge Piercy

Mami says, mid-shift at the factory we were told
no more late buses. 11 p.m. clock-out,
the payphone line long as women called
to wake someone.

Mami says, I did not want to bother Papi,
eyes & legs tired from driving the old
& handicapped along back roads, some young
to clinics. I walked home four miles,

my purse on my left. In my right hand,
I held a knotted sock heavy
with quarters. Other nights,
a switchblade.

Tongues

for Adrienne Rich

Whenever I write in my journal, I am whole.
I don't have to choose between my four tongues.

In which language do I dream? It depends.
Am I teaching or making love?

Mi lengua materna sigue ardiendo.
My mother tongue still stings, burns.

Condescension smells the same among monolinguals
& island Ricans who compliment my accent.

Hilde Domin: Heimat in der Luft. Yes, Hilde,
my home lives in the air, en mi lengua materna.

1995. Flying to Iran, I read Neruda in Spanish, my lips
still swollen from my husband's kisses in German,

unsere Liebessprache, our love language, the bridge
between us foreigners loving in a Dortmunder Hochhaus.

Say my full name the right way. Your tongue,
your voice – both instruments – won't break.

Bones

for Catherine Sasanov

Not enough drugs. Papi felt the surgeon's saw, fire through bone.
No wonder he lost his sleep. Papi feared dreams mired in bones.

One of John Hammond's treasures, a sailor's skull. Whose grave
was robbed? What price did Hammond pay for his desire for bones?

"Lord, enter my body through these broken whispers. /Death ... gorged
on my family. TB only picks at my bones." Prayers you write in stone.

Island Puerto Ricans' lament: Where are the graves of our loved ones?
Hurricane María hurled winds, used sea water as fire. Now, no bones.

Don't bury me whole in Oak Grove. Bury my ashes near a library.
My spirit will read a forest of words, battle your desire for my bones.

Fairy Tales

for Anne Sexton

Women's voices shared stories die Brüder Grimm transcribed, not
                                        mere fairy tales.
My college students gasped at the true versions. Blood-
                                        smeared fairy tales.

The fairest daughter ate dirt & died. The darkest daughters, 11 & 9,
                                        sold to cook
& clean, their monthly visits home to deliver their wages.
                                        No ears for fairy tales.

Sexton wrote: "her china-blue doll eyes,/ open and shut./ Open
                                        to say,/ Good day,
Mama/ and shut for the thrust/of the unicorn." Girl-woman
                                        seared in fairy tales.

We read that the dwarfs in Snow White were children, growth
                                        stunted by work
in coal mines, dust making their voice gravel, no time
                                        nor tears for fairy tales.

The dictionary stamped "obsolete" gave me coded words for the
                                        world I hid
from my teachers. They praised my poems, dark
                                        with fear, as fairy tales.

huracán san roque   1893   pr

for Patricia Smith

        door broken again
        luisa's mother prayed
        soothed her with secret stories

guabancex
        angry woman spirit
        makes the winds & water
        move

        the terrible twins
guatauba & coatrisque
        thunder & flood
        come before & after her

guabancex
        casts houses
        to the ground
        uproots trees

        they say
        the eye
        of every hurricane
is her face

        the Spaniards
        know nothing
        name hurricanes

guabancex's fury
        after saints

anima

for Tracy K. Smith

Does this man who preyed on this child stop
having a soul? Does it die? Return to the sea
or sky? Is it hollowed out with a knife,
the meat of it, buried in someone's backyard?

What of the soul of this child he harmed?
How does this child wade through a wound,
stop feeling silence as heavy as a man's body,
stop from drowning in this life?

space between us

for Margaret Szumowski

Mentor, friend, poet, you believed in me, closed the space between us.
Memories slide off and die. Alzheimer's grows the space between us.

My Swedish host mother refused to cross Checkpoint Charlie with me.
At 18, what did I know? The blue passport showed the space between us.

Border patrols in Bulgaria ignore me, your wife, cuff you off the bus.
I return to Germany, wait for your call to close the space between us.

Speeding down 91, cars swerve to miss turtles, their genetic memory
moving them across two lanes, shells slow in the space between us.

Ready to birth my only child, I call my mother to help. She recoils
at the thought of such bloody witness, her "¡No!" a space between us.

Walls

for Edwina Trentham

We lived side by side in a duplex. The only daughters
        among boys, we had fathers who spoke with fists,
mothers who loved too much to leave. Once my father
        discovered how easy the shed was to climb
for a boy to kiss me through my window, he moved me
        to the attic room with no door. My family
of books followed in milk crates. Through the thin wall
        of the duplex, you and I rapped codes to check in
after another bad night, rapped times to escape
        to meet boys we thought we loved. I remember
how you slid across the slanted roof, slipped
        through the tiny ceiling window, makeup and clothes
in backpack, snuck down to my brother's room
        over the shed – and disappeared.

freedom   1894   manatí pr

for Natasha Tretheway

the nights   luisa couldn't sleep   the heat of her sisters' bodies
sticking to her   left & right   her brothers' sighs   papá's
serrucho
snores   mamá's dream whispers   the coquis' symphony

mamá grande   76   lit a white candle   whispered chants
not in spanish   with phrases that ended   libertad

once   luisa asked mamá grande   for the meaning of her words:
10 babies mean freedom   10 babies baptized, freedom
10 babies who live   beyond TB & hookworm, freedom
10 babies   no longer slaves   taste libertad

Made in the USA
Middletown, DE
11 January 2019